Wordsmith Workshop

Write & Publish
Your Novel

A common sense approach
to writing and publishing a novel

By Greg Past

First edition, 2015

Wabana Press
36219 Shoreview Drive
Grand Rapids, MN 55744

greg@gregpast.com

Table of Contents

Introduction..5

The evolution of storytelling 7

Benefits 9

Getting started.......................................11

Plot & Symbolism...................................14

Characters 17

The setting 20

Write, rewrite…rewrite..........................22

Sell your writing 24

Self-publish..27

Summary 31

Introduction

This is a practical guide to writing and publishing a novel.

I recently published my first novel, *The Wabana Deception.* It was a daunting task. When I started writing, I had no idea what I was doing. I simply wrote. I was stubborn and determined to complete the task. As a result, I encountered and overcame many difficulties. It took over a year to finish my first draft. When I reviewed the completed manuscript I found discrepancies in the story line and typos. I rewrote the manuscript several times. Through trial and error, I honed my writing skills and refined the process of writing a novel.

I understand the problems a new author faces. Throughout this book, I share examples of my experiences so anyone writing their first novel will understand the problems and difficulties they are face are not unique. It is our task as writers to overcome these difficulties and complete the task. Writing a novel is an attainable goal.

By reading and following the steps in this book you have embarked on your quest to become an accomplished, published author. Good luck on your journey!

The evolution of storytelling

There is something magical about telling a story. Picture an ancient tribe sitting around the fire after hunting and gathering all day. There were no houses with electricity and running water; just a simple group of huts surrounding a communal fire pit. What did they do for entertainment? Someone told a story.

Great stories originated in this humble manner. Writing was non-existent. Books came much later. Stories were passed from generation to generation by word of mouth. The subject of the story could be anything. The task of the storyteller was to capture the imagination of the audience. The story had to be entertaining. Did the storytellers exaggerate? Of course, exaggeration creates drama and generates interest. Over the millennium, these basic concepts of storytelling have remained the same. The method of delivery has changed dramatically.

Primitive stories were recorded on cave walls. A series images depicting the hunt told the story of life's struggles in tribal communities.

A great improvement in storytelling was writing. A few educated people would write on leaves or vellum scrolls. Examples of scrolls from antiquity exist in museums. The ancient Greeks collected these scrolls forming the great library of Alexandria.

Eventually the idea of compiling these scrolls into books with pages and a cover became popular. There are many examples of monks transcribing ancient religious texts using beautiful calligraphy and detailed artwork.

The printing press made it possible to mass produce books. This innovation made books available to the average person.

As technology improved story tellers gained the ability to reach huge audiences through radio and eventually television. At the same time movie theaters proliferated.

With the advent of the internet, cell phones and mobile devices, we can stream audio and video. Multimedia productions have become a sophisticated art form.

Yet, one thing remains the same, storytelling. The teller of stories must capture the audience's imagination. He or she must take their audience on an emotional roller coaster and resolve the story in a manner that will make the audience eager for more.

Our goal is to fascinate the world with our story!

Benefits

The benefits of writing a novel are many. Here are a few good reasons to tell a story in the form of a novel.

1. Writing a novel is an accomplishment. It is estimated that only one person in one hundred that starts writing a novel will complete the task. You become a remarkable person by writing and publishing a novel. You establish yourself as a thoughtful and purposeful individual.

2. Writing a novel is a learning experience. Your story must be believable. In order to accomplish believability, you must be an expert on the subject of your novel. In many instances you will research your subject extensively.

3. Writing a novel is an adventure. It is an experience that will enrich your life. Many people spend a good portion of their life in front of the television watching other people pursue their careers. When you write, you spend your time productively exploring new ideas, new worlds. The possibilities are limitless

4. Writing a novel satisfies your need for creativity. Writing is a satisfying activity. When you finish writing for the day, you have accomplished something. It makes the rest of your day go better. You look forward to writing again tomorrow.

5. You establish yourself as an expert. Because you have written about a subject you establish yourself as an expert. Your readers will consider you knowledgeable and may even seek your opinion or expertise on matters pertaining to that subject.

6. **Writing is a great hobby.** You can take your hobby, writing, with you wherever you go. All you need is a word processing program on your laptop, tablet, cell phone or just a pencil and a piece of paper. The sky is the limit. You can strive to be a great novelist. You may travel the world researching settings and subjects. Maybe you would just like to write for your enjoyment. There choice is yours.

Getting started

Where do I start? That is a good question. It is easy to tell friends and family that you are going to write a novel. One of the most difficult parts of writing a novel is getting started. The problem is there are so many things to consider. The expectation is to sit down and write a complete manuscript. In reality, your goal is to write a first draft.

Start writing!

Recognize that in the beginning, you do not possess all of the skills necessary to write a novel. You do possess the ability to tell a story. A novel is a long, complex story. Do not let shortcomings stop you. Writing a novel is a lot like learning to play a musical instrument. When you first start playing the instrument it does not sound like music, with practice you learn to play your favorite song. After several years of practice you master the instrument.

Writers write. Set a time to practice writing every day. Writing two hours a day or more is ideal. I suggest you wake up two hours earlier than usual and devote that time to writing. If morning is not convenient for you, select a time that is convenient for you to write. Try to write at least 500 words a day.

If you write 500 words a day, in 200 days you will have written 100,000 words

If you write five days a week, 200 days equates to 40 weeks.

You do not need to know how the novel ends to write the beginning. You do not even have to start at the beginning. Just write about whatever comes to mind; start writing. In 40 weeks you will have a respectable first draft.

When I started writing my novel the first thing I wrote was a short story about a trip to the island on Wabana Lake. There was a local legend that Chief Wabana was buried there. I made up a story about searching for Chief Wabana's grave. That was the beginning of my novel. I continued to work on my novel every day. I found myself thinking about the storyline at different times during the day. Ideas for my story came to mind while I was working on other tasks. I added characters as I developed the story. When I finished the first draft, I had 110,000 words, I was ready to edit and rewrite. That manuscript did not resemble the original short story I wrote. There is nothing in my novel about an island in Wabana Lake. The story evolved as I wrote.

Start writing!

Your story will evolve as you write. Do not expect your first draft to be the finished product. Rather expect your first draft to be a manuscript you will edit, improve and polish. Strive to complete your first draft.

There are many resources available to help you develop your writing skills. There are books and courses devoted to writing. There are many courses online. There are instructional YouTube videos. There are videos on YouTube in which accomplished authors talk about how they got started. Take every opportunity to improve your skills

Plot & Symbolism

Plot

Go to any search engine and type the question, 'How many plots are there?' The common answer is seven basic plots. The theory is all stories are variations of seven basic plots.

So, what is a plot in a story? A plot is a literary term that describes the series of events that make up the story. It is also known as the story line or plotline. Every novel has a plot. Novels also have subplots which add to the story.

Plotting is a subject in itself. There are books and videos explaining how to plot a novel. There are courses about plotting. You may choose to plot your novel prior to writing it. The plot must keep the reader wondering what happens next. It must make the reader want to turn the page. The dramatic action must draw the reader into the novel building tension until the end or the novel when the tension is released.

It is not necessary to plot your novel ahead of time. All of us have an intuitive understanding of how a story is put together. It is a good idea to have terms like plot so we have a common language for discussion. However, let us remember terms are just terms; we do not want to become so bogged down with terms that we do not write our story. After you begin your novel, your most important goal is to finish it. As a result of working on your story daily, you will develop a plot and subplots.

In my novel, *The Wabana Deception,* the plot is the protagonist's quest to find out what happened to her mother. There is a subplot where the protagonist explores her sexuality with a friend/lover. This could be called a romantic plotline. The plot and subsequent subplots developed as I wrote.

When reading a novel; pay attention to the plot and subplots. Now that you are a writer, it is easier to look at the novel you are reading critically, as a novelist would. Pay attention to how the author combines different scenes to tell the story. Note how the author creates interest; ending a scene or a chapter by leaving the reader to wonder what will happen next. Read books by several different authors; each author has their own character and style. Strive to develop a style for that works for you.

Symbolism

A symbol is defined as something that stands for something else. This definition is vague and can be difficult to understand, yet we use symbols all the time. Also, it should be pointed out, that the same symbol can have different meanings in different situations.

Think of a bouquet of flowers. You may give someone flowers to express romantic intentions for that person. The flowers are a symbol for your love or admiration. You may bring the identical bouquet of flowers to a funeral. The flowers are a symbol of your sympathy for family and friends that lost a loved one. The same bouquet of flowers has a different meaning in different situations. But in each situation, the flowers express simply what is difficult to express in words. We can use the same concept in our novel.

In The Wabana Deception, the protagonist is searching for the mother she never knew. All the protagonist has is a charcoal drawing of her mother smiling. She keeps the drawing on her wall and fanaticizes about her mother. In the beginning of the novel she imagines her mother is smiling at her. She thinks the smile on her mothers face is expressing a secret happiness they will share together when they meet. Throughout the novel the protagonist slowly finds out what her mother was really like. In the end, the protagonist thinks her mother is laughing her. The charcoal drawing is a symbol of the protagonist's mother.

There are many resources available explaining the use of symbols in literature. Explore these resources as you write your novel. Experiment with the use of symbols in your writing. Whether it is a dove, a rose, a jewel, a drawing or some other symbol, use that symbol to express simply what is difficult to express succinctly in words. Remember a symbol can be interpreted in many ways. Use symbolism judiciously.

Characters

What makes a character interesting? Is it their personal appearance? Is it their personality? Is it the car they drive? All of these attributes contribute to how we perceive an individual. A character is interesting because of their actions, what they do.

In order to make our characters interesting to our readers, their appearance and actions must hold the readers attention. Our readers must have empathy and sympathy for our characters and our characters must be believable.

Empathy is defined as 'feeling into'--the ability to project ones personality into another person to more fully understand that person. We want our readers to understand how our characters feel, to identify with our characters. The reader should know what it is like to 'walk a mile in their shoes.'

Sympathy is feelings of pity or sorrow for someone's misfortune. Sympathy derives its meaning from Latin and Greek words meaning "having a fellow feeling." Typically, in the beginning of a novel our protagonist faces tragedy. The reader should be sympathetic with the protagonist. The reader should share feelings the protagonist experiences because the reader has similar feelings.

Verisimilitude is the appearance of being real or true; believability. Our characters, our story must have the appearance of being real or true. The key word is appearance. We are writing fiction with the intention of entertaining. We may exaggerate. Our protagonist's intentions are so pure and noble it is tragic. Our antagonist must be eviler that evil. Yet, we do not want the make the character unbelievable by carrying these traits of good and evil to a ridiculous level.

In the beginning of my novel, *The Wabana Deception*, the main character is a high school student. Her name is Lomasi. Her mother disappeared before Lomasi was old enough to remember her. Lomasi never knew her mother. This is an example of using an orphan's tragic circumstances to gain the readers sympathy; to draw the reader into the character and ultimately the story.

Reading further we discover that even though Lomasi's mother abandoned her, Lomasi obsesses over her image. She personifies a charcoal drawing of her mother. In the beginning she thinks of her mother as pure and wholesome. Over the course of the novel Lomasi finds out her mother left her to become an exotic dancer. That her mother used drugs and alcohol and she was promiscuous. We are in her corner hoping for the best outcome. We are empathetic.

I would like to point out again that when I started writing my novel, the story was about an island in a lake where a Native America Chief was buried. I developed these ideas because I worked on the novel daily. I read daily. Because of these daily activities I found myself thinking about my novel and developing ideas. My novel evolved into the story of Lomasi over time because I worked at it and I was determined to finish.

Start writing! In the beginning use yourself as the protagonist, someone you know intimately.

As your novel progresses that may change. Read a little bit every day. While you are reading, pay attention to how the characters are developed. Make a mental note of techniques the author uses to make the characters interesting. Think about how you could use the same literary techniques in your story.

Also, when developing your characters, think of them as friends. Think about future novels while you are writing this one. You may want to use the same characters in your next novel. Your readers will become attached to your characters and will enjoy reading about them again in your second novel. Your readers will think of these characters as old friends.

Remember, it is our intention the reader to become emotionally involved in the story. To speculate how the story will end. The reader should anticipate love interest. We want our readers to stay up late finishing our novel; to leave them with an appetite for more. We want the reader to be sympathetic and empathetic with our character.

The setting

Your novel will be a series of scenes that tell your story. The scenes need to be anchored in reality in order to make the story believable. Your characters and dramatic actions need a setting, someplace for the story to take place. It is very likely as you develop your novel there will be several settings.

How do we make the setting seem real to the reader? First and foremost the setting should be real to the writer. The reader should be left with the impression that the author is intimately familiar with the setting. The easiest way to accomplish this is to select a location that is familiar to you.

Use all five senses including smell to describe the setting. We experience the world around us through our senses. Using all of the senses will give your reader a richer experience while reading your work

If you want to use a location which is not familiar, visit it. Pay attention to the details. Take pictures of the areas you are interested in describing so you can refer to pictures when you write.

Another option is to use an imaginary setting. Use your creative abilities to invent a location that suits your story. You may be writing fantasy. Perhaps your story demands a location that does not exist in reality. An author can invoke artistic license to create their own setting.

Metaphor can be useful when describing your setting. A metaphor is a thing regarded as representative or symbolic of something else. Here is an example of metaphor:

The sun shone like at golden medallion in the sky

Comparing the sun to a golden medallion will help paint the mental image of the scene in your readers mind. The use of metaphor should not be restricted to setting; it can be useful in all aspects of your writing. Experiment with the use of metaphor in your writing.

When I started my novel, The Waban Deception, the setting was Wabnana Township and Grand Rapids, Minnesota. As the story grew, I wanted the protagonist to go to school at the University of Minnesota, so that became another setting. Also, I needed someplace for the antagonist to grow up. I chose Miami.

People often read to escape their every day life. Selecting an exotic or romantic location for your dramatic action to take place can make the novel more attractive to your reader. One of the benefits of writing and publishing a novel is the business aspect of being an author. Once your novel is available for sale at a bookseller you have established a business. All or some of the expense incurred creating your novel may be tax deductible. That means if one of your settings is Florence, Italy; your travel expense may be tax deductible. Seek the advice of a competent tax advisor to determine what expense you may deduct.

Remember; get a clear picture the scene in your mind. Paint that picture with words for your reader.

Write, rewrite...rewrite

Congratulations! You have completed the first draft of your manuscript. Now it is time to edit, rewrite and polish your story. Your goal is to captivate the reader; make your story so compelling that the reader cannot put the book down. Your novel should be so interesting a publisher will contact you requesting the complete manuscript after reading the first few pages.

To start, read your novel critically. Read it from the perspective of someone who picks your novel up for the first time. Correct spelling and grammatical errors. Ensure there is something in each chapter and section to pique the reader's interest.

After I completed my first draft, I reviewed and rewrote it to ensure congruency. I made the story up as I went along. Because of this, many things I wrote in the beginning had to be changed so the story was consistent beginning to end. I strove to perfect the technique of leaving the reader hanging at the end of each chapter so they would be motivated to read further.

Get a bunch of post-it notes and find an empty wall. Describe each scene briefly on its own post-it note; then outline your novel scene by scene sequentially on the wall. Go over the order of the scenes ensuring you have the in the optimum order to create and hold your readers interest. Experiment; see if you can create more drama and suspense by changing the order of the scenes.

Ask friends and family to review your manuscript and give you their opinion. Keep in mind that not everyone you ask to read your manuscript will actually complete the task. It is a big favor to ask of someone. Be happy with any feedback you receive.

Another alternative is to join a writing group. Search online for groups of people with similar ambitions. You can meet with other authors to discuss your story and exchange ideas. Some groups will review a chapter of your book and critique it. There are many benefits to meeting regularly with a group of like minded individuals.

It may be you are so familiar with your manuscript that even though there are grammatical and spelling errors, you do not recognize them. There are editing services where accomplished writers will edit your manuscript correcting grammatical and spelling errors for a fee. For example Writer's Digest, www.writersdigest.com, offers a menu of services. It is called 2nd Draft Manuscript. The will critique your manuscript, your query letter and provide any number of services that can be helpful. This is one of many services available. Search online for the service that best suits your needs and budget.

Sell your writing

Imagine selling your novel to a large publishing company. They design a cover and mass produce your novel. It is distributed to bookstores worldwide. The publisher embarks on an extensive and expensive advertising campaign. You go on book tour, cash huge royalty checks and sign autographs for adoring fans.

In reality, most of us will need to develop a strategy to sell our writing. I will discuss three approaches you may wish to explore. The first approach is contacting a publisher directly. Tue second is finding a literary agent to represent you. These two approaches will be discussed in this chapter. The third approach, self-publishing, will be discussed in the next chapter.

Writer's Market is a book that will be invaluable to you in your quest to be published. It is an annual publication containing information about publishers, literary agents and a myriad of information designed to help sell your writing no matter what you write. You may purchase a copy of Writer's Market from a bookseller or there are copies available in most libraries for your use. It is also available in an online format.

Writer's Market provides examples of query letters; letters written to an agent requesting representation. If you are a poet or would like to write magazine articles there is information in Writer's Market for you. It is worthwhile to spend some time browsing through a copy to become familiar with the different services available.

If you wish, approach a publisher on your own, without the help of a literary agent. Research the publishing company to determine if they currently looking for new authors. Ascertain the genre they publish. For example, if you wrote an adventure novel, it would not make sense to submit it to a publishing company that specializes in religious materials. Use Writer's Market to do your research. Another idea is researching in a bookstore. Look for books similar to yours and make a note of the publisher.

Once you identify a publisher, determine the best person to contact. Write a cover letter and send your manuscript. Follow up with a phone call or email. Be persistent.

It may make sense to seek representation through a literary agent; someone who specializes in selling novels to publishers. This will allow you to focus on what you do best, write. The literary agent will charge a commission for their work, a percentage of your sales.

If you wish to find a literary agent, use the Writer's Market publication to find one that works with the genre of book you have written. Subscribing to Writer's Market online can be most helpful. The entry for a literary agent's firm will have a link to their website. The website will list submission guidelines, if the are currently accepting new authors and additional information regarding their firm. In most instances they provide an email address. You can write your query letter in email format. Many of the agencies will ask you to paste a sample of your work in the email. Again, you must be persistent. There are many agents to query. If you do not find one on you're the first time, try again.

Approaching a publisher directly or finding a literary agent, may not work for most of us. It is worthwhile to try this approach. The rewards can far outweigh the effort if you are fortunate enough to be published and your novel becomes popular with the reading public. In reality, the number of novels that are published is small compared to the number or authors that submit their work. It may be practical for many of us to pursue self-publishing.

Self-publish

There are many possibilities to consider when self-publishing your novel. I suggest you research options on the internet. Find the option best suited to your needs.

I chose Createspace by Amazon.com to publish my manuscript. My choice was based on cost and distribution. It is possible to publish a paperback on Createspace with minimal or no cost. Your novel will be distributed on Amazon.com and related websites. You may also publish music and film with Createspace.

Paperback

Createspace is a print on demand publisher. When a copy of your paperback is ordered, they will print and ship it to the buyer. Createspace will credit you with a royalty. There are no up front charges. There is no minimum order of your book. There is also a Createspace community you can join that will provide help with the process of publishing and marketing your book.

It is relatively easy to publish your paperback using Createspace. You simply create an account, user name and password, on their website, www.createspace.com. You upload your manuscript in file format. Your manuscript will be checked for errors. There is an interior reviewer that will allow you to preview your book. There is a Cover Creator which allows you to select from several predesigned covers. You modify the cover adding pictures and text. You can also proof your novel online. All of these services are free. If you choose, you may publish your novel at no cost. You may purchase copies of your book at cost. A royalty account is setup for you. Royalties can be deposited periodically in the bank account of your choice.

eBook

After you publish your paperback on Createspace you will be given the option of publishing your novel in eBook format. There will be a link to Kindle Direct Publishing. Follow the prompts on their website and publish an eBook formatted for Kindle. It will be distributed for you at no cost on Amazon.com and related websites. When purchased, an eBook can download it immediately. A royalty will be credited to your account with Kindle Direct.

Smashwords is another publishing service that will publish your manuscript in eBook format at minimal cost. Smashwords is partnered with Barnes and Nobles, Apple, Kobo and Sony and more. Their website is www.smashwords.com. Follow the online instructions. Your eBook will be published and distributed to major eBook distributors with little or no cost.

Book Cover

You can choose between using a template to create your book cover, creating your own book cover, and having a professional design the cover for you.

Createspace has several cover designs to modify for your book. There is no cost for this service. You may use the same cover for your eBook. If you use a Createspace template, simply select one you like best. Add a title, pictures and a description of your novel. You may choose to furnish information about yourself as the author.

If you would like to create your own book cover, search the internet for information. Research and select the method that is best suited to your needs.

I chose to have a professional design my book cover. It cost $150 and reflected my ideas for the design. The designer worked with me, making many revisions, to create a cover for my paperback; then modified it for publishing an eBook.

ISBN

An ISBN is required to publish and distribute a book. Createspace gives you four options for an ISBN.

Free Createspace-Assigned ISBN: Create space will assign an ISBN to your book at no charge.

Custom ISBN: Set your own imprint and be listed as the publisher. The cost at this time is $10.00.

Custom Universal ISBN: Set a custom imprint while keeping your distribution and publishing options open. The current cost for this service is $99.00

Provide Your Own ISBN: If you have an ISBN that you purchased from Bowker® or through your local ISBN agency, you can use it to publish your book through Createspace. You must also enter the imprint name associated with the ISBN.

There are other methods for obtaining an ISBN. Enter Bowker in your search engine. You will be presented with many options for purchasing an ISBN.

Description

Write a short description of you novel for the book cover and to post on the internet. You may choose to add your biographical information.

Summary

Congratulations! You have finished this book and are well on your way to a rewarding writing experience.

The benefits or writing are many. You are exercising your creative abilities. You are accomplishing something that very few achieve, writing and publishing a novel. Writing can be a hobby, a career or anything in between. The opportunities are endless, it is up to you to decide what you would like to accomplish.

Writing is inexpensive. All the tools to write and publish a novel are at your disposal at minimal cost. All that is required is you pay your dues by spending time writing and improving your skills.

The most important thing is to get started. It is easy to become discouraged and quit. Writing a novel is not an easy task. Remember you do not need to possess all the necessary skills to begin writing a novel. You can learn as you write. Write daily. Your novel will progress in small steps. Every day and week and month your writing will improve. Take baby steps and gather momentum.

A plot is a literary term that describes the series of events that make up the story. It is not necessary to plot your novel in advance. You can make the story up as you go along. Once you have completed your first draft, you can polish and refine your manuscript into a finished product.

It is what your character does that makes them interesting, their actions. Strive to make your characters believable to the reader. Pay attention to methods other authors use to make their characters interesting and adapt those techniques to your writing style. Experiment with symbolism. Your readers should be sympathetic and empathetic with your characters.

Your story needs a setting. The setting must seem real to the reader. Either select a setting that is familiar to you or research a setting. One of the benefits of writing is you can travel to interesting places to research for your novel. Since you published your novel and it is available for purchase at a reputable reseller, your travel expenses may be tax deductible as a business expense. Consult your accountant or tax advisor for advice before taking any tax deductions.

Do not expect your first draft to be the finished product. You may have to rewrite it several times. Have your friends and family read your manuscript critically and get their input. Join a writing group to get the opinions of other authors regarding your novel. For a fee your manuscript can be professionally edited.

Try selling your manuscript to a publisher either directly or through a literary agent. The Writer's Market can be a useful tool to identify publishers and literary agents.

Self-publishing your novel can be a viable alternative to approaching a publisher or literary agent. There are many services you may use to self-publish. It is worthwhile to research your options to find the one that best suits your needs. Createspace will publish your paperback and eBook and make it available on Amazon.com with minimal cost.

Kindle Direct and Smashwords will publish and distribute your eBook at no cost.

I would like to thank you for buying and reading this book. If you have any questions or comments, please feel free to send me an email, gregory.j.past@gmail.com.

Other books by Greg Past

The Wabana Deception--a novel

Reflections by the Lake--a collection of
poems

www.ingramcontent.com/pod-product-compliance
Lightning Source LLC
Chambersburg PA
CBHW031336040426

42443CB00005B/371